I am this is.

I Am This Is
Copyright © 2016 by Emily Rose
All rights reserved.
Written By: Emily Rose
Illustrated By: Emma Mulvey

Thank you for helping me discover who
I Am. This Is for you.

Foreword

Amidst the chaos and darkness of today, where so many appear to have lost their way, the words of Emily Rose emerge as the North Star on a dark and dangerous night.

This 17 year old, African American, adopted as a very small child, and brought into the warmth of a loving home, by a Caucasian, New England adoptive mother, amidst the wealth and comfort of Marin County, California, one of the wealthiest counties in the country, has managed to accomplish and now share with us - amazing insights from both worlds.

As a voracious reader of the classics by Orson Welles, F. Scott Fitzgerald, and many others, Emily would often consume a 500-page book in a single weekend. She simply, could not get enough.

Although she finds much of what she reads often

to be cut and dry, she really appreciates the undertones that connect with her, as she attempts to find both herself and her way in an overbearing society; one in which she doesn't quite fit into.

Her love of both prose and poetry has led her to writing, and her insights are astonishing. At the age of 17, she has lived in both worlds. The world of physical wealth, and the poverty of the spirit of a 17-year old African American who finds that much too often the comforts of a Marin County home disappear as she exits the gated property her adoptive mother has provided her. Through the breath and depth of these insights, Emily Rose allows us to live in both of these worlds – simultaneously. You do not want to miss it!

Holman Turner

The Instrument
I do not write
Words lace themselves together by
    means of my ink stained
    fingertips

This day felt like a revolution

And I'm still learning how to
    disassociate happiness and
    stagnancy
And I'm still learning it's possible for
    me to change my view on the
    world
I'm still learning who I am
And more importantly I'm still
    learning how to teach myself to
    be better
I'm still learning to teach myself how
    to be happy
And how to be happy with my
    happiness without carrying some
    twisted version of survivors guilt
I'm still learning to be thankful of the
    past instead of resenting the
    people who dwell there
Trapped because they know I'll never
    let them out of their cages
but
Why should I even hold them within

me?
I need to set myself free and I think it starts with letting go and letting in
It might start with accepting this
> internal change and recognizing it as something good instead of something that takes away my identity

Because
Who wants to be rooted in sadness
> and anger?
Who wants to internalize all the hate
> and melancholy they've ever felt?
I've always prided myself on being a
> realist but I think it's finally time to be realistic
Realists don't feed off depression and
> bath in rage
And I think I'm still learning when it's
> time to perform a sage cleansing in my mind

i just want to make art that moves people

I've never really been healthy and
maybe that's why all of this is so
scary
This is more than just a 3 AM
sleepover screaming bloody
mary
I've been crying bloody murder
Tissues pressed against my thighs
Headphones pressed against my
eardrums maybe this bass can
drown out my heart beating
wildly in my temples
Because mind over matter is starting
to sound more like Christian
Science and I've always been
better at English
Skipping church on the weekends to
read about bad religions and
equating God to styrofoam cups
And when my thoughts get to be too
much I've followed in the
footsteps of my family in the

form of red wine and choose
      a life of teenage angst in the form
      of red lines
Determined to be swallowed by the
lies I told myself at night. . .
"If I ignore it for long enough
everything will be alright,"

And if I happen to fall into the path of
      luck I'll be able to use my
      suffering as a means to write and
      connect to someone who
      felt like they had no one to
      understand their plight

I am angry
Or maybe it's enragement
Because I've been stuck way too long
    in this fucked up engagement
Living like an outsider trying to get in
    No. Living like a snake
    uncomfortable in my own skin
Like maybe this time when I shed my
    colors might be different
And maybe this time my lighter scales
    could spark an interest
Because dark girls very seem to be
    trending in the cyber district
Still we attempt to empower ourselves
    but are shot down in an instant
In favor of white girls with the
    same   damn   statistics

I am sick

Of living in this world of ignorance
This world that discredits my mental

brilliance
And instead focuses on my afro's
   existence
This world that acts like from the
   slums I need deliverance because
   it can't get past my melanins
   pigment

I am tired

Of living for a white man's desire
Of only my butt being admired
Of only my hair being accepted when
   it's run through a flat iron

This is discrimination

Its modern form that thrives in our
   nation
Its form that celebrates my hips
   gyration
That consumes my sexuality with a

fierce predation
But rejects my mentality like it spews damnation
    I've come to live in a bubble of desolation
Feeling forced between goals of exploitation or assimilation
Choosing a life of black characterization or white sophistication
This is asking me to dismember my identification

This is torment

Asking I revise myself for your discontent
Demanding I reinvent until I reach your consent
But never taking into consideration the way I resent
You

All the things you put me through
The way I now see myself as taboo
The lies you once told me I now
    know to be true
And the growth of my confidence
    you can seamlessly undo

This   is   The System

Forcing me into a position of
    restriction
But damn you if you think I'll
    continue to be a victim

This is a movement

Not a problem that needs a solution
But an evolution of minds ready to
    burn down your blueprint
    and make our own
A generation of minds ready to take
    your throne and make your

corruption know
Ready to tell the world your actions
    we do not condone
And for your sins you must begin to
    atone
For it is you who has made our lives a
    battle zone
Everyday we fight to eradicate words
    like red and yellow bone
Fight to stop our movements being
    compared to a cyclone
Fight to stop being treated like clones
Fight to stop our appearance being
    indicative of "crime prone"

This is civil war

Only without the civility
Fighting with neurological weapons
    but without any dignity
Slaying us with rounds of oppression
but still avoiding the publicity

The way you keep this underwraps
    continues to be a mystery
Somehow you are able to paint our
    children with delinquency
Able to strip our professionals of any
    authenticity
Able to trap our minds into captivity

And all in the name of our ethnicity

But this is not a war that you can win
Because strength does not grow from
    the color of your skin
It grows from the power you hold
    with in
The years you spent fighting against
    lies of sin
The years you spent hiding bullet
    holes with a grin
You may think you have won the war
    but really it has yet to begin

No

This is the end

On this day a truce I can no longer extend
To you because your ignorant mind I cannot comprehend
That my black is beautiful
And it is more than just a trend
It is my mind and my soul and for that I will not be condemned
So come resurrection day I'll be going up and you'll be going down

Funny to think because you're the one who's white and I am the one who's brown

Scarification
Your words lacerate my silences into
　　a thousand gilded ribbons s

For the first time in three years I
    didn't cry on my birthday
I didn't lay in bed with wet cheeks
    counting down the seconds until
    the night passed into August
    15th
I didn't feel all my hope swell inside
    my lungs before being
    expelled with the light of pink
    wax candles
And for the first time in three years I
    didn't wish to stop loving you
Because I don't anymore
But I am still in love with symbolism
    and poetry and I am still in love
    with the symmetry of you
    leaving my heart and my mind
    exactly a year after you broke me
    for the last time
And I'm proud to say that I am
    no longer healing
I am healed

And I'm better off knowing what it
 feels like to have kneeled in
 false pews and prayed to false
 gods
But
I still find myself kneeling
I still find myself praying
Feeling a little less religious
Feeling like my old uncertainties are
 giving way to staying

And there's nothing else I'd rather do
at 2:43 on a Sunday morning
than listen to him breath life into
lyrics

And I don't think I was ready for you
> before
You were too real
Too innocent
And I felt like corruption incarnated
> I felt like every wrong decision I
> ever made was all that defined
> me
And God I felt so lost and you seemed
So found

I'm not quite sure what made me so
    Black and Blue
In a sea of bright white and soft
    yellow I felt myself sinking
    towards the bottom
No one wants to see a dot of Black
    and Blue
        and I felt my colors fading
My Blue seeped into green as the
    overwhelming sea took over me
It couldn't stand my discrepancies as
    white foam soaked into my skin
Green and grey but my colors were
    still estranged from this sea
I still don't quite fit in but I'm closer
    to what it wants me to be

It does not matter if you put your
    hands up
It does not matter if you are innocent
(you are life) Threatening
black lives (Don't) matter

I see I am Black Gold despite its truth
    you've tried to burn out of me
Now these scars on my back are
    giving birth to branches bursting
    out of me
This tree of my being has grown from
    roots practiced in
freeing   trapped human   beings
See I absorb their wisdom like water
Words leading with me in tow as
    natural
        As breathing
Using me as the instrument for their
    speaking
So know this Truth I'm unsheathing
So sharp with meaning
Will leave you bleeding but
        Heart still beating faster
Society might tell you different but
    you don't no master
You don't need no pastor
You were not cast in someone else's

play stop living like an actor
>And put down that castor oil
Girl
Your hair is beautiful in coils
Skin as rich as soil
Not an insult but an indulgence in its
>natural abundance of creation
Girl
You were the foundation of
>civilization
Before a single adaptation a single
>mutation
Your DNA gave birth to these days
Don't let our Truth be set ablaze by
>the system's deceptive rays
Let your burnt scars amaze you
>they'll grow roots that betray the
>Black Gold you contain and feed
>the branches that allow your
>family shade

I am deflective humor and angry hips
I am tired eyes and hungry lips
I am a country at war but a people at peace
I am contradiction
I am singularity
I am Emily Rose Todd
I am the epitome of hipster popularity writing novels and watching Netflix and spouting about feminist radicality
I am 16
I am natural hair
I am light skinned dark souled
I am a 1960s child that graduates high school in 2016
I am the daughter of a white mother and no father
I am an adoptee, yes my single parent always wanted me
I am confusion
I am a trap

I am improv jazz music
I am a delicately coordinated tap
I am a circle you try to fit inside a
 square
I am unshaven legs
I am braided hair
I am swollen lips
I am painted toes and glittered eyes
I am ears closed shut from too many
 lies
I am smiles masking fear
I am smiles hiding pain
I am a brain that feigns memory loss
I am angry hips
I am loving arms
I am damaged heart
I am tired eyes
I am girl who eats too much pizza
I am girl who stays up too late
I am girl
I am woman
I am 16

I am black
I am American
I am financially rich
I am emotionally poor
I am overly passionate
I am passively psychopathic
I am contradiction
I am singularity
I am Emily Rose Todd

continuously.
receiving.
transforming...

teeth shattered from the chatter of twitching gums.

- The Anxiety

thoughtlessness.

- The Cause

and I hope one day I can find comfort
in hope the same way I find
security in hopelessness

(and I have)

Heart broken every time but never quite surprised
These eyes have seen too many lives claimed by the force that's supposed to save them
But
This system is a lie and most don't realize...
    The legacy of slavery is still alive
The repercussions of living with dual identities has left us with an internal drive of independence
Cut into us with the first restraints on our limbs
Revived by each new cut to mental freedom
But
Suppressed by people prone to treason
In this country everyone is supposed to be equal

So explain why the Civil Right's
    Movement needed a sequel

Titled: Black Lives Matter
    Captioned: To All People

Added commentary at the bottom of
    the page: "Still all I see are men's
    names."

No one's ever been able to do this to
    me before
Make me shut down so completely
    that all I can feel are the tremors
    ripping through my muscles and
    goosebumps crawling over my
    skin
I'm freezing

But it's August

Maybe I knew I was in love with you
when I stopped wearing
sunglasses when you were
around so nothing would come
between our eyes

And for once I'm freezing in August
But it's only the nighttime air

And it's ironic
That the moon would rather glow at night than share the blue sky
And it's ironic that the tides can only swell in the north as they wane in the east
And it's ironic you claim it's only the laws of nature when humans have been defying the laws of evolution for years
And it's ironic we've become better at helping ourselves than each other
Forgot our intertwining roots in pursuit for the sun
But our branches wouldn't grow stronger without the rain
And soil couldn't quite nourish the same without all its living creatures
And it's ironic you told me,
"Things have to die to feed the Earth."

"But baby that's not death. It's Rebirth."

I never believed in religion
Until I touched your hands and your
    knuckles weighed like rosary
    beads wrapped around my
    fingers

I hope this uncertainty is only my
   subconscious rebellion against
   my conscious decision to put my
   life in a positive place

And I'm not angry at you anymore...
I'm grieving

　-family

I am terrified
But be warned this is not another race poem
This is not angry scared black girl VS.
    Insert - racist white men
    Insert - police brutality
    Insert - institutionalized racism
    Insert - the massacre of my black brothers and sisters
But this is not another race poem
But I am still terrified
Heart threatening to burst out of my chest
Drenched in cold sweat
Hands shaking
Stomach churning

Do you remember what it feels like to find yourself in love?
Do you remember what it feels like to skip the fall and find yourself landed in his sprawled arms

Do you remember thinking the
    heavens must've known you
    were afraid of heights?

Because I remember being terrified of
    the thought of throwing myself
    off a cliff twice
Thinking a second chance wasn't
    worth a roll of the dice
I was terrified. And ready to settle for
    my high up view of the lights
    until I missed myself falling
Landed straight into being
I could've never imagined his green
    lights up close had the power of
    freeing
I only ever imagined myself fleeing
    from the possibility of pain
    despite thinking of myself as
    strong
And it's not until now
    Writing on this page

I realized how wrong I really was
Because how can you be strong if you
      run from the weight room
If you never challenge yourself to
      bloom in places you thought
      were forever frozen
If you allow yourself to stay broken
      because it's easier to shut down
      than share emotion
This writing on this page is here to
      challenge the ocean of terror I've
      been swimming in for too long
I'm here to grab hold of the reaching
      lyrics in his songs
I'm here to take a cession from my
      political aggression and step out
      of my box and onto this page to
      release my realest confession

I am terrified of his love and all that it
      means

I'm terrified of the way I feel my heart
    slipping into his like a glove
To the point that I don't even know
    what to think of myself
This girl that used to keep her heart
    tucked away up on a shelf but
    never on her sleeve
I've found this boy's honesty has
    given my emotions permission to
    roam free

And I'm terrified that I've never felt
    more at ease
And I'm terrified that he even
    appeases the terror in me